THE WILD DAYS

NLP
1972 TO 1981

by
Terrence L. McClendon

Illustrations by Marni Taylor
Cover illustration by Tom Killion - Last Winter in Santa Cruz
Book design by Kasrynne Huolohan

Copyright © 1989 by Terrence L. McClendon
All rights reserved. No part of this book may be reproduced in any form without the written permission of the author.

Library of Congress Catalog Card Number: 89-062912
ISBN: 1482650312

*Dedicated to
Claire Kathleen*

Contents

Foreword		i
Introduction		iii
Chapter One	- Santa Cruz Bridge Trolls	1
Chapter Two	- The Winter of '72	5
Chapter Three	- Gestalt Class	9
Chapter Four	- Five Feet In The Air	17
Chapter Five	- Fritz	21
Chapter Six	- Food Stamps	25
Chapter Seven	- Virginia	29
Chapter Eight	- Parts' Party	31
Chapter Nine	- War Days	35
Chapter Ten	- Mission Street	39
Chapter Eleven	- Meta Model	43
Chapter Twelve	- Devra On The Cross	45
Chapter Thirteen	- Cream Pies	49
Chapter Fourteen	- Eye Accessing Cues	53
Chapter Fifteen	- Milton	57
Chapter Sixteen	- Acorn Hollow	61
Chapter Seventeen	- Lake Tahoe	65

Contents

Chapter Eighteen	-	Leslie and Virginia	69
Chapter Nineteen	-	5-Tuples	73
Chapter Twenty	-	don Juan	77
Chapter Twenty One	-	White Horse	79
Chapter Twenty Two	-	Xray Eyes	81
Chapter Twenty Three	-	J Ward	85
Chapter Twenty Four	-	Mind Reading	89
Chapter Twenty Five	-	Tying It Together	95
Chapter Twenty Six	-	Taking It To The Road	99
Chapter Twenty Seven	-	NLP Volume One	103
Chapter Twenty Eight	-	The Untuple/Spinning Out The Belief Strategy	105
Chapter Twenty Nine	-	The Wedding	109
Chapter Thirty	-	DOTAR	113
Chapter Thirty One	-	This Town Is Too Small	117
Chapter Thirty Two	-	Operationalising NLP	123
Epilogue			129
About The Author			131
Bibliography			133

Foreword

NLP: The Wild Days is the story of John Grinder's and my adventures during the formative days of NLP. It's not only the story of the outrageous things that Grinder and I did 25 years ago; it's also the story of the spirit in which NLP was founded, has grown, and continues to evolve.

That spirit is basically the belief that anything is possible, and that it's the human mind that makes it so. This idea is much more common and widely accepted now than it was back then; in those days, people used to express the impossibility of something by saying, "There'll be a man on the moon before that happens." Of course, in 1969, putting a man on the moon lost its power as a metaphor for impossibility!

Grinder and I never accepted what most people assumed about the limits of human beings anyway. We always felt that humans were capable of much more excellence, creativity, and success in all kinds of endeavors-than most people believed. The growth of NLP, and its application to fields as diverse as physics, pilot training, and sales-vindicates the approach we took.

After all this time, it's still exciting for me to look back at those early days. The perspective of 25 years shows us that while what we were up to back then may have seemed wild and crazy, what's really outrageous, at any time, is to reach the boundaries of human knowledge or capability and not be afraid to move beyond them.

Terry McClendon has admirably captured the spirit of this singular adven- ture that NLP offers people. More and more people all over the world are realizing that neither deep space nor the ocean are the "final frontier"; the real frontier is to gain control over cognitive evolution, so that individuals, groups, nations, and all humanity are truly prepared for the stern challenges that lay ahead.

Terry's book brings back a lot of pleasant memories of funny things that happened during those early NLP days. Of course, Terry's recollections of the now-long-ago past may not match in every detail those of other people who were there. In some cases, they don't match mine exactly. But that's not the point. What he has captured, beyond dispute, is the spirit of adven- ture that gave birth to NLP and that continues to energize it. As long as that spirit survives, NLP will continue to push out the boundaries of human potential into uncharted, but very stimulating, waters.

Thank you, Terry

Richard Bandler

Introduction

The Wild Days is a personal account of the historical development of Neuro-Linguistic Programming and its two key developers, Richard Bandler and John Grinder. The author traces the development of NLP from its preconception in 1972 thru to its maturation in 1981. This book is a first hand account of the training seminars and wild stories of NLP's two key figures. It also discusses the key figures of the core groups of the early days, their relationships and career developments.

The serious student of NLP will find this book a useful addition to your collection of metaphors about NLP. All others will find it fun. With its twenty seven illustrations it is the book that all the visuals have long waited for.

This book should be kept readily at hand for those precious moments in your morning duties and on the bedside table for a spicy piece of entertainment before retiring.

Enjoy, Terry

Chapter One

Santa Cruz Bridge Trolls

Richard Bandler in 1972 was a student at the University of California at Santa Cruz. The city of Santa Cruz, population 40,000 in 1972, sits languishly on the Monterey Bay directly across from the historic state capital of Monterey. The temperate climate of Santa Cruz and its unique environment afford you the pleasure of its many beaches and cool redwood groves.

The occasional bridge troll can still be found under the Water Street bridge, one of the last strongholds of the American Hippy, where a tourist is confronted with River, Water and Ocean Streets and wonders which way to the beach. The home of The Hook at Pleasure Point and Steamer Lanes, the surfers mecca. For those in the know about crystals, pyramids and tarot, Santa Cruz's stature is equal to that of the Bermuda Triangle, Boulder Colorado and other high energy windows to the universe. The home of Alfred Hitchcock, Jay Silverheels of the Lone Ranger and Tonto, Shirley Temple, Frank Herbert, Gregory Bateson, Baba Ram Dass, Santana, The Doobie Brothers, Tom Smothers and more.

The University is tucked away amongst the redwood groves overlooking the city of Santa Cruz and the Pacific Ocean. Its peaceful atmosphere lends itself to almost anything except serious academia.

Richard used to walk around the university campus looking like he just came home from a street fight on the back streets of San Jose. His hair was longish and he sported a goatee. He was rarely without his knife on his hip. Now everyone knows that anything could happen to anybody at anytime, in nowhere. However I believe Richard used to take that literally even in the quiet calm atmosphere of the university.

Richard Wayne Bandler grew up in San Jose, California. You could liken his childhood to that of the "cats and jammer" kids - ragamuffins around the block. At one time Richard's family owned a restaurant and he used to hang around and watch his mother cook which gave Richard a natural ability for cooking. On the odd occasion that I would visit him at his Bonny Doon house he has cooked some fantastic meals.

Richard however, wasn't able to fully appreciate the benefits of his own cooking. During his escapades as a child he received a wound to his stomach which he led me to believe was a knife wound. Part of his intestines were removed so he wasn't able to digest some fresh vegetables. He is a great believer in meat and has a bias for a certain French restaurant on Ocean Street in Santa Cruz.

Richard graduated from Freemont High School and entered Foothills College in the Los Altos Hills. After two years he transferred to the university at Santa Cruz where he began a major in mathematics and computer sciences, later transferring his interest to the behavioural sciences.

Chapter Two

The Winter of '72

During his student years, Richard was parading around from class to class, taking philosophy, logic, computer science and mathematics. When I would see him in a classroom he didn't seem to be at all interested in the course content.

One afternoon in 1972 in a psychology class called the "Interpretation of Personal Documents" presented by Professor Bert, Richard stood up and started ranting and raving about the practicality of psychology courses at the university. "They should be teaching something more practical for people such as Gestalt Therapy". He would get red in the face, hyped up, shout and storm out of the class room. Bert happened to be in complete agreement with Richard. He would say, "there isn't anyone at the university who can teach a practical course in Gestalt Therapy."

Richard was in an experimental stage of his career which I feel is a life long stage for him. He was very interested in a school of thought called Gestalt psychology which focuses on bringing immediate present experience into greater clarity and increasing awareness. Richard spent many hours reviewing transcripts about Gestalt Therapy, starring a person named Fritz Perls, M.D.Ph.D, the founder of Gestalt Therapy.

He was also interested in other contemporary psychotherapies, and family therapy, a way of bringing about change in a family by working with the immediate and sometimes extended family system and developing expertise in Rolfing, a method of deep massage used to realign the connective tissue of the body.

During his student years, Richard made some of his income working at a publishing company for a person named Robert who is a doctor, lawyer and the owner of a publishing company. Bob asked Richard to edit some of Fritz Perls' transcripts and the results of that editing was Richard's first book called *The Gestalt Approach and Eye Witness To Therapy*.

Richard was quite proud of his first book. In fact he used to keep it with him at all times just to show other people. He would often have it on him personally, and kept it with him in his car so that he could show hitch hikers whilst he was driving around in his 1966 yellow convertible Chevy II SS, that he had authored a book.

Chapter Three

Gestalt Class

Being disillusioned with the activities and courses and the curriculum of the university, Richard decided to set out into creating his own curriculum. One of the advantages of being a fourth year student at the University of California in Santa Cruz was that you could develop and present your own seminar and the students who attended would receive the same credits as if they were taking a course from a full professor. Richard decided to teach a student directed seminar on Gestalt Therapy.

In the spring of 1972, Richard held his first class at Kresge College at the University of California in Santa Cruz. Kresge College was the home of the "soft sciences". It was the college that the psychology students wanted to go to because it featured a lot of "encounter group activities".

One such activity it was said to have featured was nude dinners where everyone would show up and take off their clothes and then sit down for dinner. This was known as a "growth experience" and was very popular among the first year students.

Richard's class was strictly a clothes on affair. Nevertheless Richard had a flair for the bizarre. He had a way of unveiling peoples psyche.

Richards seminar was a student directed seminar which meant that he could teach a course if he was supervised by a faculty member of the college. John Grinder had agreed to be Richard's supervisor for the course and very soon became keenly interested in Richard's approach to changing behaviour.

At that time, John Grinder was in the process of working thru the stages of becoming a professor at the University of California, Santa Cruz. He had received his Ph.D. from a college in San Francisco, where he studied the theories of the American linguist Noam Chomsky, and studied extensively the syntax of language. John at this time had co-written at least one book called *On Deletion*.

John came from a large Catholic family in contrast to Richard being an only child from a Jewish background. John was quite experienced already in using behavioural flexibility and modelling languages. He served in the military where he was classified as an interpreter, spoke several languages and participated in covert activities under the sponsorship of the United States Army. He was also accustomed to changing of identity.

On one specific operation he spent some time in Africa where he lived with a village of Africans and through a specific modelling process acquired the language of Swahili. He went via the beginnings of learning the behaviors of languages thru the process of modeling.

With John's brilliant skills in languages and already acquired skills of modelling, as well as his experiences acquiring his Ph.D. in linguistics, he bought into his association with Richard many different skills and an understanding of modelling and its application to languages that Richard had yet to acquire.

John was very active in progressive teaching techniques at the University. He even went as far as to get the university to hire *Richard* to copresent some of his courses. Back then, John's preference was for t-shirts and denims rather than a tweed coat and bow tie. He was always clean shaven and wore his curly hair longish. With his two children living with their mother, the recently separated John lived alone in Scotts Valley deep in the Santa Cruz Mountains.

In the spring of 1972, John became Richard's supervisor for the course to be held at Kresge College. John was a novice at that time in the applications of counseling and psychotherapy, so the idea of supervisor Was a bit of a misnomer and a question of who supervised who.

John with his brilliant modelling skills from linguistics in conjunction with Richard who had the experience in behavioural modelling skills and his knowledge in the new contemporary systems of psychotherapy, formed a relationship which later on proved to be exceptional and beneficial to both. A relationship that set the foundations of a methodology that was the driver for an evolution of human communication.

Richard began the performance of his duty as a seminar instructor at Kresge College. His first class was Gestalt Awareness, a typical class in this new system called Gestalt Therapy. The classroom consisted of a carpeted floor with several pillows around the outside walls. Two pillows were strategically placed in the middle of the room. The students would come in and sit down in somewhat of a circle. Richard would arrive, take off his knife, put it beside him, put out his props, including cigarettes and a box of kleenex tissues, and ask, "Who would like to work first?" At that point it would be a contest between the students of who could convince who, of the importance of fixing their problems first.

Now the term 'working' in this sense meant that one individual would go into the centre of the room and sit on a pillow and would then start a technique called "Shuttling Psychodrama and Confusion". Richard Bandler would play the Gestalt Therapist, cigarettes and Kleenex tissues at the ready and discreetly direct a student to become aware internally and externally of whatever they were seeing, hearing or feeling at that moment in time.

The technique would then usually evolve into what was called an open chair technique where the person in the middle of the room would imagine a person in an open chair and begin a conversation with this imaginary person about some unfinished business or conflict that the student would want to work on.

The technique would continue until such that the person with the assistance of Richard was able to resolve their problem or they reached an "impasse". Impasses were generally achieved when the person realized that they might get what they wanted and so they make a decision that they do not really want to change after all. This results in what is known as being stuck. Impasses were sometimes able to be resolved by using group members to play out designated roles having to do with the persons conflict. This procedure is often called psychodrama, and is where most of the fun came in you were given the opportunity to do outlandish things in the name of personal growth.

Often Richard would direct a student to intensify a feeling and that feeling would then lead them into a historical search where they would go back to an earlier unresolved experience. Richard would then use this technique called psychodrama and assist the person in having a dialogue with parts of themselves or their imagined family members until they could integrate the conflict that had arose. The technique would often evolve into a "busting" thru their blocks and having metaphorical breakthroughs.

When considering the building blocks of NLP you first need to consider the two individuals who generated this incredible methodology. The personalities of Richard Bandler and John Grinder. NLP is as much an attitude as anything else. It was once written in a psychology magazine in the United States that NLP was Richard Bandler and John Grinder and that it was their personal charisma that achieved the results not the NLP techniques. The attitude of NLP is more overtly demonstrated in Richard's training and therapeutic personality. The attitude is one of GO FOR IT! It is one of assertiveness which is often confused for aggressiveness. It is one of lust for life, experimentation and if that doesn't work, do something different.

Richard was conducting a workshop at the university, and also conducting several external workshops and classes throughout the Santa Cruz area. Some of these were weekend courses, some were night courses. It was through these courses that Richard developed his incredible perceptual skills. He principally used Gestalt Therapy, some deep massage techniques, Reichian Therapy, and then later on Family Systems Therapy primarily from a model which Virginia Satir developed.

Chapter Four

Five Feet In The Air

One of the weekend workshops that Richard taught was a Gestalt Group in Soquel, a small town just outside of Santa Cruz. The venue was at Bob's house, one of Richard's employers and was settled in nicely amongst the redwoods. After the "who wants to work" ritual was completed the shuttling and psychodrama exercise would begin and the person in the "hot" seat would begin with "Now I am aware and comment on their internal and external awareness.

In one such exercise I ended up blowing out some metaphorical blocks. Richard had me first take a deep breath and take hold of his wrist. As I squeezed his wrist I was instructed to breathe out and say no at the same time. I did this and apparently Richard was not satisfied with the result so he had me kneel on the floor and as he bent over me to hold me down, I repeated the breathing and shouting nooooooooooooooooooooooooooooo.

The result was quite astounding. I lifted Richard up and tossed him five feet in the air. Richard then asked me what I was aware of and I said that I wanted to do it again. He just looked at me with a smile and said, "You're done," and so went the Gestalt Groups of that era.

Richard promoted his own groups around Santa Cruz thru word of mouth. He was very good at what he did and often had to limit his group sizes. He was aloof, in fact I often wondered if he actually knew the names or had any contact with the people in the groups outside of the group areas. Richard was not really considered a loner but he had few choice friends that he associated with.

He was presenting groups that were quite different from what was normally being presented around the university area. There was a lot of groupy, groping activities going on in the "Encounter Sessions" of the era. Richard's groups had very little to do with that kind of activity as Richard was quite a different kind of personality.

Chapter Five

Fritz

John Grinder in his role as course supervisor, became aware of the brilliant behavioral skills of Richard Bandler, and the suggestion was that if Richard taught John what he did then John would help him model it and one thing led to another.

They chose some of the geniuses in behavioural communications of the current era. With John's background in linguistics, the most logical place to start was verbal communication. They listened to and watched audio and visual tapes of key people in the fields of communications and therapy. Some of these were Fritz Perls, Virginia Satir, and later on Milton Erickson M.D.

John brought to the stage of NLP the dual characters of the striving professor of linguistics and the covert operations officer who worked for the army. In his formal training, he used deep trance identification to increase his ability to blend in with his immediate environment and had experimented with modelling in the learning of languages.

The idea of "parts" began to play a key role in our training workshops. Specifically the polarities of what was called the "top dog" and "under dog" models of Fritz Perls' Gestalt Therapy. Perls pointed out that the top dog-underdog split is one of the most frequent splits in the human personality. The top dog is the righteous conscience. He always says what you should or should not do. The top dog attempts to lecture, urge and threatens the underdog into "good" behaviour. The underdog is the placating, accommodating manipulator who says, "Sure, I promise," or "I agree, if only I could..."

It is interesting to note that at times Richard and John demonstrated very unorthodox therapeutic techniques and it is also important to realize that, thru the entire training process of the development of NLP John and Richard had the extraordinary ability to create the connectiveness and the understanding which is necessary in a powerful, congruent therapeutic environment. They had the ability to be completely and absolutely with the client/student in dealing with any situations that would come up.

All experimental exercises and techniques that I am aware of were done with the utmost sensitivity and systematic skill that you would expect in a very high quality experiment. The results achieved were not always predictable and were sometimes counterproductive; however, with that magical skill of utilization, they could put whatever resulted into a positive and useful framework.

Chapter Six

Food Stamps

Looking back, it was laughable in terms of the financial output for the students at that time. Considering what seminar fees are today, $25 a month in 1972 was considered a big rate although Richard was open to taking the equivalent rate in food coupons from the impoverished student who did not have the cash.

The supervision course in the spring of 1972 developed into several training workshops and programs, which were primarily conducted by Richard, and later Richard and John, and were attended by students mostly from the University of California.

Now there has been many things said about the original group of NLP. This obviously is purely a matter of where you want to start. When did NLP first begin? At that time who was a part of the original group? For historical purposes, I will put the record straight. The original group of NLP would be around the modelling stage of the Meta Model Groups that were held at Frank Pucelik, Leslie Cameron and Judith DeLozier's house in the Santa Cruz Mountains.

Some of the group members were Ken of the Mission Street house, Devra, David, Judith Delozier, Leslie Cameron, Paul, Steve, Frank Pucelik, Byron Lewis, myself and squeaking in towards the end, Robert Dilts. For all intents and purposes, these are the people who seemed to hang around the longest. Kind of like workshop followers. There were others of course and, if any of you are out there, I'll put your name in volume two.

Chapter Seven

Virginia

Richard met Virginia Satir, or so he said, at a cocktail party. Virginia was a social worker who was very keen on the family systems approach to family and couple therapy. She developed a model of communication and family therapy that she called "Conjoint Family Therapy".

Over a period of approximately two years, Richard was introduced to several communication techniques by Virginia. In fact he thought that she was so good at what she was doing that he used to fly around the United States and visit her training programs, to attend and learn everything that he could about how she worked.

He was primarily an audio specialist at these workshops and he used to tape and assist in the videoing of many of her training programs.

In one of these training programs Richard was introduced to a therapeutic tool called the "Parts' Party". Along about 1972 Virginia developed this model as well as another model called "Family Reconstructions". Richard was very excited about these models. They are very active and very profound in their results. Richard was also very excited about how Virginia worked and we would relish in his story telling about her uncanny perceptions and skills.

Chapter Eight

Parts Party

Briefly a parts' party is conducted in this manner. There is a guide who supervises the party and a star who is in it for therapeutic value. The star is chosen and comes to the front of the group. He or she then chooses ten characters, famous characters, and gives each character a description. The star then chooses ten people out of the group who will play the role of these characters. The characters can be famous actors, business people, politicians, historians - whatever they choose. The role could be the ability to be aggressive, the ability to be successful, the ability to understand or be sexy.

So, ten people get chosen, then they get programmed for their roles. They are then instructed to go into a separate room with a supervisor, who goes along and instructs them to interact as if they are at a party.

Consider now there are ten people in a cocktail party, each individual is playing out the role that was designated to them by the star. The instructions which they are next given is that each individual character is to work at taking over the entire party. To use the resources of their part, to get the rest of the group alongside and take over the dynamics of the party.

At times conflict arises, it is at that point the guide freezes the group and they all hold their postures. The guide points out the conflicts to the star, and it is at that time the star begins to come aware of the conflicts, which are arising in their own internal world.

This process goes on sometimes for a number of hours, each one of the individuals of the party is trying to take over the party, until at such time the entire party is together. Sometimes during this process the parts are transformed and they become other parts as they integrate with each other. So the parts, individual parts, and the polarities of the individual are then integrated. There are ten separate parts, or five sets of polarities, with different conflicts going on at the same time.

The results of several hours of interaction are that all of the parts are transformed, integrated or connected in some positive way to another part. It can get pretty mad at times and people do get a bit testy with each other. Whether it has ongoing or permanent therapeutic value, I really don't know. They certainly were fun though.

In attending several of these groups which Richard conducted, I have become quite acquainted with the parts' party. Richard probably gave hundreds of parts' parties during his career.

Richard then evolved into the next dimension, Family Reconstructions, revisiting old learning's and looking with new eyes. Making this possible is the job of the guide, often played by Richard. The star is seeking illumination through revisiting his or her childhood within the context of the whole family. The objectives of the family reconstruction is to realize your own parents' personhood, to reveal the sources of your old learning's and to pave the way to finding your own personhood.

Richard did a very powerful family reconstruction for John Grinder in one of the training sessions in which John uncovered a very enlightening part of his personal history. It was experiences such as his family reconstruction that helped hook John into the therapeutic process. He attended several of Richard's groups.

Richard taught John personally how the therapeutic process evolved. John was a student at many of the groups before he became a supervisor himself. Richard and John then began to co-lead groups. The groups that they were leading had a little bit to do with Gestalt Therapy, a little bit to do with what Virginia Satir was doing, and a little bit to do with what John Grinder and Richard Bandler were making

Chapter Nine

War Days

During the middle seventies when the Vietnam War was coming to an end there were a lot of anti war demonstrations going on throughout the US. The University of Santa Cruz was not much different from other universities. Protest marchers would get together to march against policies of the USA in Vietnam whenever they could find the opportunity.

One protest march that stands out in my mind was an organized march that took place on the streets of Santa Cruz. One of the organizers of this march was none other than John Grinder. John was a bit of a radical at this time in his life with his t-shirt, denims and longish hair. He took on the responsibility of organizing what he called "infinity groups", which sounds like something left over from his military service days. These groups consisted of three people, who were to look after each other as they went thru the protest march.

John and his troops were stationed at the intersection of Highway 9 and Mission Street to blockade the highway. To counter the blockade were police officers from the Santa Clara Tactical Squad with their batons and tear gas.

So imagine if you can the infinity groups marching down the road, towards the blockade with everyone reassuring each other and John telling everyone to stay together and watch for your infinity group members!

Meanwhile Richard Bandler was doing a personal protest of his own on the streets of Santa Cruz Mall. In his Super Sport Malibu he was roaring up Front Street, the main street of Santa Cruz, driving so close to the Santa Clara Tactical Squad that they literally had to jump out of the way of the approaching car. The police were diving off the road left right and center. For awhile after this episode Richard and his yellow Malibu SS kept a very low profile around Santa Cruz.

Looking back, it is this type of scenario which truly reflected the approach to life and attitude of the two key players in NLP.

Chapter 10

Mission Street

A new dynamic occurred in the relationship of John Grinder and Richard Bandler at one of the groups held at Mission Street in Santa Cruz. The Mission Street house was taken over by several students who were attending the university. The group was initiated by a person named Ken who continued his association with NLP and later went to work with the Santa Cruz Community Counselling Centre before going on to bigger and better things. Some of the attendees were David, Devra, Frank, Ken, Leslie, Judith, Richard, John, Paul, Katherine, Debbie, myself and others.

The skills we were learning were couple counselling and some family sculpture stuff and a little Gestalt thrown in here and there. One group night Richard was teaching couple counselling techniques. The primary people involved in the couple counselling session were Frank, Judith and Leslie. Frank was going thru some separation conflicts with Judith and he was living with Leslie. Frank was a student at the university and lived in student housing with Leslie who was also a student. Frank wanted his cake and to eat it too. So there was some problems between Frank, Judith and Leslie, and Richard was the facilitator.

What I remember about Frank was he seemed to be very nervous. Not surprising considering the situation. He had very short fingernails because he used to chew them a lot. Leslie was your classic, voluptuous blonde. She responded dramatically to her association with Richard and went thru some very powerful changes in a relatively short period of time. Richard had a very strong influence on her. Judith seemed to keep in the sidelines. Her involvement from what I remember was minimal, as was John Grinder's who was the ever present overseer, progressively changing from a passive to an active instructor.

The emotional shifts and expertise of skill in working with three people in this situation were mind boggling. However Richard pulled it off and Frank, Leslie and Judith reached an amicable understanding.

It was at the Mission Street groups that we first began acquiring our information gathering tools that were later to become the meta model patterns. The foundations of the information gathering tools began with the how, who, and what questions from the Gestalt framework, deleting that unspoken question, why.

We used to get yelled at and sometimes bopped on the head for saying why. In a very therapeutic way, of course. The meta model patterns and some of the counselling techniques were derived from watching and listening to video and audio tapes and transcripts of Virginia Satir and Fritz Perls.

The dynamics were very interesting during that time, as group participants worked together and shared emotional issues. Richard was introduced to Leslie Cameron and John was introduced to Judith Delozier. Later on Leslie became more and more interested in the therapeutic process and stuck around for further groups. Judith never seemed keen on therapy. She was studying religious studies at the time and continued her interest in that area.

The weekly group fees were going up and we were now paying $50 a month. It's now 1974 and the groups are beginning to evolve. One, probably the most interesting of these groups, was a group that was held in the Santa Cruz mountains. A primary forum of this group was Gestalt Therapy with some couple and family systems counselling techniques using Virginia Satir's work as a basis of development.

The importance of this group was that it was the group that was the experimental grounds for the meta model. The group took place in a house just outside of Scotts Valley in the Santa Cruz Mountains. It was a large wooden mountain house which lent itself very easily to a large group meeting. Frank, Leslie and Judith all lived there. Frank was able to resolve some of his conflict, and he was living with Leslie in the house, and Judith was in attendance at the granny flat. It was during these groups that Judith became more involved with John Grinder.

Chapter Eleven

Meta Model

The meta model developed thru trial and error over a period of several months. The group members were the trials and errors. The application of the language patterns was a Gestalt Therapy context. We were taught one meta model pattern a week.

The meta model was designed as a process tool to complement other forms of information gathering skills and adapt very easily to other forms of counselling and psychotherapy, and in the near future, business and educational applications. However some people were getting the wrong impression of what the meta model was all about. Robert Dilts and I had a course participant show up at one of our introductory seminars having heard that the meta model cured schizophrenia. He was very adamant about proving us wrong. We quickly dispelled these claims and got on with teaching NLP.

Richard originally supplied the therapeutic expertise and John the model using his linguistic background in transformational grammar as a starting point.

The structure of the group proceeded in this way. The group members would pair up, one person would be a people helper and the other would have the presenting problem. We would go into various rooms and gather information concerning the presenting problem and how it fit into the person's model of the world. We were given some theory on deep structure and surface structure relationships and the distinctions between the map and the territory.

We were taught one meta model violation a week. We went in and practiced the questioning technique, came back and then were meta modelled by either Richard or John to determine if we were able to fill in all the pieces of the person's world model. The outcome of this particular technique was to be able to get a full linguistic representation of an individual's model of the world.

Chapter Twelve

Devra On The Cross

The meta model group was probably the most dynamic of the groups that were held throughout the Santa Cruz mountains or should we say productive, in that, the end result of this group was the meta model. A year later it was put into a book titled *The Structure of Magic I.* Probably the most significant part of this group for some was the ending. Richard and John liked to end their groups with a bit of pizzaz. They generally liked to hold a party to give presents to the students. The ending of this group coincided with Christmas. So there was a group Christmas party held around the end of 1974.

First I'll have to set the stage for you. It was evening about 8 o'clock and everybody was sitting around in a circle waiting for the festivities to begin. Both Richard and John were in attendance for this particular gala occasion, as were Judith, Leslie, Paul, Frank, David, Devra, and others.

Richard was in the middle of the room and he would say, "Who would like to have their gift first?" Devra would always like to get hers first. She suggested she get her present to begin with and was very happy and excited. The events began to unfold. First, Devra was sent out of the room and ten people were chosen out of the group to serve as actors and actresses, of which I was one. We were all given white sheets to wear and candles to hold and we walked out to the side deck of the house, and were we surprised! Because on that deck was an eight foot tall cross like the one that Jesus was crucified on.

We were instructed to stand around in front of the cross and hold our candles in front of us. Devra was led out blind folded and was then tied onto the cross. John then put some lighting fluid at the bottom of the cross and proceeded to set it ablaze. Devra at this time began to smell smoke and was wondering what was going on. She started sounding anxious about the situation asking, "What is going on?". Richard asked her if she would like to have her gift now. She said she would and so Richard took her blindfold off and gave her a knife which she could then use to cut herself off the cross.

To this day I don't think that Devra has ever forgiven Richard. I have heard that she is still plotting on how to get back at him. Richard did have a serious discussion with her after about how she could learn from the experience, however I don't think she was listening.

Chapter Thirteen

Cream Pies

A certain aura then prevailed over the group. We began to wonder about the nature of these "gifts". The next gift was given to me.

I was taken by Richard into the bathroom and asked to take off my contact lenses if I had them in. Since I had a nice shirt on I was instructed to take that off also. Then a smock was placed over me. Lastly a blindfold was placed over my eyes.

Richard took me on a blind walk. This seemed to be pretty basic stuff to me, something out of psychology class 1a at junior college, until I fell into a hole. Richard then said, "You have to be very careful and to see where you are going because you can only have a glimpse of where you are going." He then pulled the blindfold down for a half of a second.

I was then taken up and placed on the deck where the cross was still standing. I was instructed to sit cross legged, then told that there were ten people in front of me who were my devotees. I was then to chant "OM" to these people. You see I got pretty good at using the meta model, in fact I thought that I was hot shit. Perhaps a bit arrogant.

I continued to chant once and then twice and then was instructed to be louder. In a third attempt, when my mouth was open wide, Richard and John threw cream pies right into my face. The cream went up my nose, in my ears and all over my hair.

Richard then took my blindfold off and asked, with his best Virginia Satir voice, "Are you O.K.?"[11] I looked at him and laughed and laughed. It was probably one of the first times that I had a really deep belly laugh.

We then went back into the house and further gifts were given out. The party that evening was quite a wild and memorable occasion.

The Christmas party was the end of an era, and the beginning of NLP. During that Christmas some of the group members were introduced to eye accessing cues. Covertly of course. Richard had a habit of teaching indirectly thru demonstration. The Christmas party marked the completion of the meta modelling group. Little did we know that Richard Bandler and John Grinder were staying one step ahead by experimenting with eye accessing patterns and predicates.

Chapter 14

Eye Accessing Cues

Rumour has it that eye accessing patterns were discovered in this way. One of the Gestalt Therapy sessions that John and Richard were conducting developed into the "open chair technique". One of them noticed that the person on the one hand was looking up and using very visual predicates, like, "You can't see what you are doing" and, "Why don't you look at me when you talk to me." Then she would change chairs, look down right and respond with feeling words like, "1 feel that we are losing contact and drifting apart." One therapist looked at the other and said, "I wonder if they actually see pictures when they use visual predicates, and get feelings when they looked down and to the right." The other said, "You'll never get me to believe that."

Shortly after the meta model group started, I had the opportunity to visit Richard about a relationship problem. It was at that time that Richard showed me the name on his new office which was "Neuro-Linguistic Programming." The model had a name. Cards were also printed up with MM for Meta Model which was later to become the logo for Richard and John's publishing company, Meta Publications.

Very intensive experimentation and modelling was the order of the day at this time. The crux of the model was that what ever works, works! The old rules about the warm, empathic and genuine therapist went out the window, and in its place a model developed called, "if what your doing isn't working, do anything else."

The NLP seeds which grew and later flourished are beginning to germinate. During this time the idea of the parts, based on Fritz Perls topdog-underdog and Virginia Satir's model; the concepts of reframing which developed through the integration of the Gestalt Model, the elaborate reframes of Virginia Satir's parts' party and the use of symptom substitutions in hypnosis all contributed to the model of NLP. Some NLP techniques developed as an evolution of these basic models. However the techniques should not be confused with the model itself. NLP is about modelling, not therapy.

The genius of Richard Bandler and John Grinder has been their ability to take any act or behavior and to be able to model it in a way that it can be taught and incorporated in other people. This is infact what they did with the brilliance and genius of Fritz Perls, Virginia Satir, and Milton H. Erickson. They often had us doing deep trance identification with these people at some of the workshops.

Chapter Fifteen

Milton

Gregory Bateson who was a neighbor of Richard's, suggested John and Richard visit Milton. They made several trips to Phoenix, Arizona where Milton lived and spent many hours talking and taping Milton's sessions. Milton quite a character himself. With two bouts of polio, being tone deaf and color blind, you would think that there wasn't much of a person there. You only have to see him once to feel the tremendous personal power that he harnessed.

With Milton you inevitably did more listening than talking. Milton taught through his stories. He spent hours each day telling stories about his clients and his family. You would fall in and out of trance continually. It was helpful to bring a tape recorder with you if you wanted to make sense out of the sessions with him.

Richard was unable to go into trance with Milton. He didn't want to miss a thing so he would program himself for consciousness so every time he began to slip away, he would snap back into being alert. Milton invited his wife to the office to teach Richard auto hypnosis.

She began with saying, "Now I am aware of my breathing, my eyes focusing in and out, the weight of my body on the chair." Richard was in a trance in about two minutes from when she started her description of going into a trance.

The meta model is now well on its way. The seeds of reframing are germinating. The idea of representational systems with more research and wild experimentation are developing. A lot of experimentation was going on regarding accessing cues as well as researching the physiology of the eyes, ears, the tactile and visceral feeling system, the olfactory and the gustatory system and observing the behavioural correlations in the models which they had begun to recognize.

Chapter Sixteen

Acorn Hollow

Richard was currently living in an area just off Alba Road in the Santa Cruz Mountains in a place called "Acorn Hollow". The hollow is located half way up the mountain from Ben Lomond. It is situated amongst second growth redwood trees organized by nature in groves after the slash and burn logging techniques that created the timber for the city of San Francisco at the turn of the century.

There were three or four dwellings and a few sheds in the hollow with a small orchard and vegetable garden. Richard's abode consisted of a four walled, hard backed tent. It was partitioned for bathtub, toilet facilities, kitchen, bedroom, and the office. The central focus of the tent was an old wood burning stove, the only source of heat where Richard did most of his writing in the evenings which often extended to the early hours of the morning.

One of the most useful learning strategies is to teach what you have learned. John and Richard began teaching workshops having to do with therapeutic change and modelling applications of hypnosis. It was approximately six months after the meta model group that another group located at a retreat centre in the Santa Cruz mountains commenced.

This group experiment ed with the rudimentary patterns of Neuro-Linguistic Programming and also hypnosis language patterns and techniques. The groups were like party night. It was a lot of doing. We experimented with the deep trance phenomena of positive and negative hallucination, time distortion, amnesia, and deep trance identification. There were always several side "shows" going on simultaneously because group members were doing different things at the same time.

Richard, having a certain attraction for thick lipped blonds became more acquainted with Leslie and that association later turned into a loving relationship with Leslie moving in with Richard into what was called 'The Big House" at Acorn Hollow. The big house then consisted of three rooms. A large living area with an open kitchen, one bedroom and a small bathroom that functioned most of the time providing there was enough water in the well. It became a larger house as Richard and John's business began to prosper. First adding on a consulting room to see clients and play music in. The hardwood floor would be replaced by plush carpeting, antiques and other furniture would follow. When Richard moved into the big house, John moved into the hardback tent and was later joined by Judith.

The introduction of Milton Erickson brought in a whole new perception to the traditional models of changing behaviour. Many of the techniques of NLP were brought about because of Richard and John's curiousity with hypnosis. You could say that the NLP techniques are the conscious mind's model of how the unconscious mind works in hypnosis. Many of the NLP techniques such as reframing were developed because of the professional communities rejection of hypnosis. The NLP techniques were a successful attempt at bootlegging hypnosis into a form that would be acceptable.

Chapter Seventeen

Lake Tahoe

The skill of both Richard and John was advanced to the point where they could conduct several activities at one time and still be completely involved in the task at hand.

I went to visit them at Acorn Hollow with a question involving my ability to see clearly once again without the need of corrective lenses and I also wanted to understand more about therapeutic metaphor. At this time John was visiting Richard and they were having a guitar session.

Richard plays the drums, jazz guitar and piano and has a satisfactory jazz voice. John was relatively new in the music scene. His appreciation of music was very high, though his skill level on instruments had not been fully realized at this time. With his brilliant modelling skills he was able to learn to play the bass guitar from Richard very quickly.

They were rehearsing some songs that they would be playing at a workshop in Lake Tahoe. Years previously, Richard had played drums in a band at a nightclub in the Lake Tahoe area. During a session break he just picked up and left, never to return to the dregs of a musician in a night club in Lake Tahoe. The music that he and John were rehearsing was to symbolize Richard's return to the beginning of the road that led him to his current path.

I temporarily interrupted their practice session. John taught me how to use hypnosis to solve my problem about seeing and at the same time and in the same trance, I learned how to construct a therapeutic metaphor.

During the period of time that I was practicing my hypnosis techniques in trance, John and Richard continued to play their raucous music, jamming away oblivious to what I was doing. I guess they weren't going to let me spoil their fun. It was these kinds of experiences that made the novice appreciate the subtlety and skill level that they achieved when they were able to carry on multiple tasks at one time.

Chapter Eighteen

Leslie and Virginia

The groups in the Santa Cruz mountains at a retreat lodge primarily learnt hypnosis and the investigation of deep trance phenomena, positive and negative hallucination, time distortion and deep trance identification.

Richard and John operate on the premise that modelling skilled people in your field of interest was a way to learn but becoming them was even better. Several experiments were then developed to do deep trance identification with people like Virginia Satir, Fritz Perls and Milton Erickson. To begin to associate in the first person with these people and to be able to identify and utilize the communication patterns that made them so powerful.

Leslie blossomed. In one of the group sessions Richard taught her to do deep trance identification with Virginia Satir. I heard that for awhile Leslie believed she was Virginia.

were that Leslie became a better Virginia than Virginia.

Her acquired skill appeared to increase dramatically after that evening. I can safely say that I was instrumental in some of her changes. At one group session on the meta model she was the "people helper" and I was her client. At one point in our session she took me and thru me up against the wall. She said that it was the first time that she realized her personal power.

The Santa Cruz mountain group and the groups that were held at Richard's house were the development of NLP. During this time period which was in 1974 the next experiments were taking place concerning what was later called anchoring, which is the pairing of stimuli with a highly predictable set of responses.

Ivan Pavlov gained fame with his experiment involving the study of the buzzer associated with a dog's salivating response. Anchoring is a technique, which was originally brought about thru the discovery of classical conditioning. What is unique about this in NLP terms is that John and Richard developed techniques on how to utilize this information in a unique application, that was talked about in some psychology circles as cognitive behavioural therapy; which, in the context of anchoring, is an accurate description.

Anchoring is used to create or access resources and problematic states in clients. Another way to use the idea of anchors is to identify existing anchors and change their experiential significance and to be able to use them in a more meaningful context.

Chapter Nineteen

5-Tuples

The fundamental basis of NLP originated as a five-tuple A-K-0-V-Ad. Very shortly after it was changed to the current representation of a four-tuple (4-tuple). Simply meaning multiple representations. We first practiced with anchoring of polarities (opposites) and in using visual, auditory and kinesthetic anchors. We experimented with tests for integrating the anchoring techniques which was called "Jamming Anchors".

As early as 1974, individuals in these groups were not only anchoring entire 4-tuples, but they were anchoring portions of 4-tuples and submodalities and applying it to pain control and creating amnesia and pattern interruption.

Richard and John developed pattern interruption into a systematic technique for interrupting automatic behaviours for the purpose of creating leverage to enable a person to direct a client into an altered state of consciousness. We were also using various components of anchoring and 4-tuples for hypnotic phenomena such as age regression, amnesia and deep trance identification.

The primary patterns which developed out of the association with Dr Milton H. Erickson was the model of communication called the "Milty Model". The Milty Model is the inverse of the Meta Model. It provides the user with the ability to speak directly to the unconscious mind and in the hands of a skilled user, doing so without the conscious mind's awareness.

The Milty Model consists of embedded questions, embedded commands, conversational postulates, direct quotes and presuppositions, collectively termed "junko logic". In association with nonverbal pacing and leading and selective use of sensory predicates, it provides a very powerful vehicle for trance induction and utilization of an altered state of consciousness. Richard and John turned the "magic" of hypnosis into learnable procedures.

In association with Milton's work, Richard and John also came across Castaneda's books, *The Teachings of don Juan, The Yaqui Way of Life, A Separate Reality* and *Tales of Power*. From there it was an integration of don Juan's use of metaphor and hypnosis and Milton Erickson's language patterns and metaphor to induce an altered state of consciousness to create deep trance phenomena.

One of the most dynamic techniques which evolved out of the hypnosis programs was the use of the double induction. The double induction is a trance induction carried out by two people. One person speaks into one ear using complex words and language patterns to occupy one brain hemisphere and the other person speaks into the other ear using childlike grammar and language to occupy the other brain hemisphere. The feeling sensations are experienced in the same half of the body as the auditory input.

This technique was used in conversations that Carlos Castaneda had with don Juan and don Genaro. This technique was used frequently during the summing up of Richard and John's training programs as a forum for review post hypnotic suggestions for future applications and learning's.

Chapter Twenty

don Juan

The groups then took on an aura of magic and mysticism as don Juan came on the scene. There were several different experiments about the phenomenon now called "stopping the world" which was a major technique and strategy applied to Castaneda's development process. Anchoring was a tool that we were taught to stop the world, as well as other tools such as reframing techniques.

The key to success in don Juan's world was to be able to stop the world. Only then could you be accessible to power, or in Milton Erickson's frame of reference, to stop the internal dialogue. don Juan considered it necessary to use peyote (a hallucinogenic plant) to interrupt Castaneda's internal dialogue so he could achieve states of unusual reality. However, as don Juan stated peyote was only necessary because Castaneda was so rigid. There is a similarity with stopping the world (don Juan's frame of reference) and stopping the internal dialogue.

The two primary techniques that we experimented with for stopping the internal dialogue was the use of what was called jamming anchors and six step reframing. I spent most mornings doing reframing and then in the afternoons I would walk into the redwood forests of the Santa Cruz mountains, pick a remote spot, sit down and practice stopping the world. The benefits are very tangible. Including increased spontaneity and creativity, and better information and other resources.

There was much overlap in the model NLP and the model of Ericksonian Hypnosis. Many of the techniques cross over from one model to the other. We often did experiments finding out what kind of patterns were going to be the most effective in curing people.

Chapter Twenty One

White Horse

Some of the evenings in the Santa Cruz mountains were spent experimenting with and developing deep trance phenomena, in and out of trance. On one evening the agenda was to elicit positive hallucinations out of trance.

Some peoples' criteria for going into trance is to experience wild and bizarre hallucinations. My test for deep trance was to be able to hallucinate a full size live white horse. After many futile attempts assisted by group members, Richard came over to see what was going on. It wasn't until years later that I realized he performed a very slick induction on me.

Richard asked me if I could see auras. When I said no, he talked in a dimly lit room about defocusing my eyes and seeing peripherally to be able to see his aura. If you are ever around Richard in a dimly lit room, you have to be almost blind to not see his vibrant orange, red and yellow aura. From there we progressed to seeing black holes which are the vulnerable spots in people's auras.

After inducing a trance in me he asked me if I could see the white horse. I said no and he said where. I said [pointing] over there. He asked me to outline it for him and I did. He then asked me if I could see it now. As I was stroking its mane I said no. A week later I not only believed that I saw the horse, I went riding on it!

Chapter Twenty Two

Xray Eyes

Experiencing positive hallucinations consciously is fun. Even more fun can be to create a negative hallucination. Negative hallucinations are the process of taking away an object that is present. The technique developed in much the same manner as positive hallucinations. We used trance states to access resources for when we had the ability to create negative hallucinations then we developed techniques to create the phenomena out of trance.

The evening we experimented with negative hallucinations was especially fun for me as I practiced developing xray eyes. Imagine what you can do with that. Well I did, and started practicing partial negative hallucinations and of course I practiced firstly on women.

Actually it began as a joke one evening at the Alba Road training programs. We were practicing negative hallucinations so I thought, why don't I try this on women. I practiced partially undressing women in the workshop and then telling them what color their underclothes were. When you think of it, we do this activity all of the time anyway, don't we? It was all done in the name of science of course.

Negative hallucinations got to be my forte after a while although I decided to give it up one day when I was practicing taking away automobiles and it dawned on me that may not be such a useful thing to do. It scared the shit out of me actually. When I now teach the practice I am sure to include a statement of caution. You may ask, why bother to do it in the first place? Aside from the fun factor, it assists in developing and re-accessing the visual flexibility you once had as a child. Anyone who is an architect would find immediate application to positive and negative hallucination skills.

The experimenting of these techniques of deep trance phenomena kept leading to the same question. What makes it possible for people to do all of these fun things in trance and not be able to do them in a normal state of consciousness? Why do people sometimes change easily when hypnosis is used and don't change when it is not?

These questions and others led to building exercises and techniques that could enable people to demonstrate deep trance phenomena and a variety of trance states when not in a trance. Erickson, Satir, and Perls' language patterns and Castaneda's metaphors combined with classical conditioning models, came together and the synthesis which was the collapse anchors exercises, change history and reframing models.

The combination of these techniques and their historical roots led people to believe that Neuro-Linguistic Programming was a new psychotherapy. In fact Robert wrote a paper titled *NLP: A New Psychotherapy* which was the precursor to the book *NLP: The Study of the Structure of Subjective Experience Volume 1.*

Chapter Twenty Three

J Ward

I can remember one evening at the Santa Cruz mountain retreat lodge, it was a training group night, and on this night Richard and John designated us patients in "J ward". J ward was in a psychiatric hospital, where burnt out psychologists and psychiatric social workers were placed.

The specific task for each person in J ward was to take on a role that was given to them by either Richard or John. Our task was to completely identify with our role. For example with stubbornness, a person who is very stubborn had to take on the role of being catatonic. A person who was putting himself on a pedestal would be asked to take on the role of Jesus Christ and so on. We had a catatonic, we had Jesus Christ, we had Mary Magdalene and several other biblical, historical and political characters.

After the individuals were given roles, they were then taken into separate rooms where another student would put them into an altered state of consciousness using Milton Erickson's model of hypnosis and then have the person do deep trance identification with the role that they were to be playing, come out of trance and completely identify with that role.

They would then circulate around J ward. The person who induced them into a trance was then to take on the task of curing that patient using any one of the NLP tools which were available. Some of these consisted of lying congruently, using the meta model, using anchoring or using metaphor.

I played the role of suffering from the delusions of being Jesus Christ. Paul was to cure me. I was asked to take my clothes off and to put on a robe. Paul tried out various techniques including the meta model and metaphor. After circulating around the ward Jesus Christ had to fend off being seduced by Mary Magdalene and was asked to assist in the building of a house seeing he was a carpenter. I was then taken to an upstairs room and underwent further treatment.

After awhile I was tired of being Jesus Christ, so I jumped out of a two story window and to everyone's surprise entered through the main entrance on the ground floor and as I watched mouths hang open with amazement, I announced that I had returned.

The technique of stopping the world became a very significant component of being a people helper and utilizing the tools of NLP effectively. It was ingrained in us, week after week, and we were taught several techniques through the use of reframing and anchoring to assist us in stopping the world. The results were to be able to be more accessible to information and resources as they came our way.

These groups also experimented with positive and negative hallucinations, time distortion, and integration using the pattern called trans derivational search, which was later on incorporated into an anchoring exercise called "Change History".

Chapter Twenty Four

Mind Reading

On one evening in the Santa Cruz mountains, Richard and John began developing some techniques for what was later called "mind reading" a technique not often referred to in NLP workshops. The mind reading workshops were held at Richard's house at Acorn Hollow. Virginia Satir was present on the opening night, which thrilled us to no end.

The house was getting larger as Richard was becoming more prosperous and prices of the groups began to go up until we reached a peak figure of $50 per month for one of these groups.

The idea of mind reading is a pretty weird topic to teach mostly because it is so difficult to verify. Richard and John were introduced to the idea thru doing different workshops and groups in the San Francisco Bay area. They were doing some interesting mind reading on the group participants, commenting on ages, dates and places people had been in the normal course of their presentation. They were commenting accurately on individuals' personal history, their ages and their partners, without prior knowledge. They decided to do some experiments which could possibly reveal the structure of mind reading, which would then give them a model from which to teach it.

To mind read was to be able to pick up internal dialogue, sounds, pictures and words which are generated inside someone, or to be able to see a visual representation of something a person is thinking about. The simplest example is circles, squares and triangles. Having a person think of a circle, square or triangle and then being able to pick which one it is they are thinking of. Most people can choose approximately seven out of ten after twenty minutes of training.

Some of the techniques that were tried out were pacing, having two people pacing each other to see if they could read each others mind. David Gordon and myself, having similar body shapes were chosen for this task. We walked around the seminar room for half of the night looking like Mutt and Jeff, with not much happening to either one of us.

Leslie, Debra and a few others were in another office doing age regression to access memories and trying to figure out what someone is thinking. Richard was working with two people in another room doing some specific programming in trance giving them instructions to read each other's mind and, last but not least, using the phenomenon of stopping the world to become accessible to reading someone's mind. The most successful group was Leslie, Debra and a few others in the lower office.

David and I joined them as they were doing some trance work and trying to identify the subjects favorite toy as a child. It appeared like a little hologram suspended in space, just above and to the right of the top of the person's head. Pretty wild stuff.

We learned several things from these exercises. Colour and skin shade changes occurred in one or the other cheeks of the sender which would form a representation of the object of which they were thinking and the highly kinesthetic people could get the same quality information through touching the person, as information is also transmitted thru body temperature.

The visual people could see the thoughts as three dimensional holograms and the auditory people experienced mind reading thru their own auditory internal dialogue.

The mind reading exercises were very successful if they were done when the sender was able to fix solidly on one thought and the receiver could stop the world. Other peoples minds are difficult to access if you are busy paying attention to their own experience. don Juan called it self indulgence. He said " acces to personal power is stopping the world!".

The applications of the mind reading skills are pretty profound. The immediate application that I found to be useful was my work with clients. It was useful to know what was troubling them before they did. Strange images began to appear when I was practicing stopping the world when seeing clients. After a few subtle questions to my client to verify my information, we were off to solve their problems.

Richard and John would use the skills in the teaching context. They would go about answering questions before they were asked. John did a pretty slick trance induction on the night of the mind reading trials. That night stands out as one of his brilliant moments. I encountered him as I was walking from one room to another and asked him a question about the work that we were doing. He simply said, "You can't see behind you", and large holes of space began to appear in my immediate surroundings as I went into a trance............

We used age regression and anchoring often in these groups as a resource to enable us to recover the creativity and playfulness of the child, which are both useful tools for the therapist. The resources of the child were also instrumental in developing the deep trance phenomenon. We were taught several induction stories that focused on age regression and there was a strong emphasis on play throughout the training groups.

A significant event that occurred during these groups was the publishing of *Structure of Magic Two*. I always thought of *Magic Two* as a transition phase. After it came out, NLP started to blossom in its own right. (Chapter 1 on representational systems is definitely the most useful part of the book, unless you like comparison studies in communication.)

Chapter Twenty Five

Tying It Together

One of the techniques that was a thread thru most of the development process was the use of therapeutic metaphor. We learned to use therapeutic metaphors embedded in a story. However a therapeutic metaphor can be fashioned in a psychodrama or in still picture form as in an icon.

Our most commonly used metaphor was patterned after Dr Erickson's use of an isomorphic metaphor woven amongst the many stories he would tell his clients. An isomorphic metaphor is a story where the sequence of events of the metaphor match the sequence of events of a person's problem.

The therapeutic part comes in when an additional resource is strategically placed in the metaphor which directs the person to a different result. Many experiments were done using anchoring and metaphor in trance, and thru this evolved the understanding of submodalities.

The understanding of tautologies was also a pattern we experimented with. The main way we dealt with tautologies was to search out both ends of the loop and do a change history on each end of the loop. For example I could be happy if I stop smoking and would stop smoking, if I was happy. This is not a recommended approach as systematic as it was. It was too long and arduous a task.

The very early beginnings of the six step reframing model could almost be thought as a send up of the parts' party model. It began something like this. Each individual was given a quantity of ten parts and also a meta part to supervise the decision making process. The ten parts of the individual were made up of characters which they designated themselves. Very similar to the part in Virginia Satir's parts' party model.

The meta person or the meta part would facilitate the interaction or the negotiations between the parts to get a specific outcome. Later on the idea of ten parts was dropped altogether and a person could have no parts, or one part or two parts and it was open ended.

Robert Dilts was attending quite a few of these groups at this time. Robert was a fourth year student at Santa Cruz and was known as a good trance subject. Robert is a keen observer and his creative talents in writing and drawing were called upon numerous times in the NLP development years. Virginia Satir would also drop in from time to time to have a look at what John and Richard were doing in regards to anchoring and hypnosis techniques

One refined model that was developed in 1976 was a six step and two part reframing model to apply to simultaneous and sequential behaviours respectively.

Other techniques that were developed were the use of synesthesia overlaps in representational systems. A synesthesia is the blending of the senses. Each representation in one sense has a corresponding representation in another sense. For example, heat in the feeling sense leads to warm colors in the visual sense. When we speak of synesthesia overlaps we are talking about a bridge that enables you to take any content and be able to experience it in a multiple of senses. Synesthesia overlaps are represented in language by phrases such as a warm color, or a bright sound or a loud shirt.

Chapter Twenty Six

Taking It To The Road

By late 1976, individuals who had been attending Richard and John's workshops for the last three or four years began presenting their own workshops, using the techniques that they had learned. Two of these individuals, Steve and Paul, were conducting elementary hypnosis workshops. Byron Lewis and I (Byron wrote *Magic Demystified* with Frank) were conducting Gestalt, NLP and hypnosis workshops. That association stopped when Byron got a job. Then in 1976, Robert Dilts and I formed a partnership and began teaching rudimentary NLP groups in Santa Cruz.

Another person with a refreshing approach was David Gordon, whose field of expertise was therapeutic metaphor. His book *Therapeutic Metaphors* was prepared as he was going thru his Master's Degree program in San Francisco. Richard supervised him in the development of his thesis on therapeutic metaphor and David later presented it as a thesis but then put it in book form.

Richard and John were calling up university faculties throughout the country and organizing venues to promote their latest models such as the Meta Model, Representational systems and Anchoring.

They were booked out solid. Something like ninety-nine out of one hundred workshop participants signed up for another workshop after a program they conducted in Las Vegas. Their humorous approach to psychotherapy and their ability to utilize existing contexts elicited comments such as this is the best show in town.

However it was not until Leslie and Judith started presenting workshops did they really start getting a following of women. Richard and John had the adaptive skills, however the era of the feminist was not ready for the male dominance and the sometimes sexist Richard Bandler and John Grinder. Leslie also gave them the Virginia Satir caring approach that was very different to the detached hurry up and humorous approach. Leslie was good and solid and appealed to those content people who needed to walk thru everything before they feel they have learned. She and Judith appealed to many people who could not grasp the subtleness of John and Richard's presentation.

Everybody was on the road. Robert and I began teaching throughout the US in 1977 and developing introductory and intermediate NLP workshops. Our first workshop on the road was promoted by Steve Stevens, now Steve Andreas in Boulder Colorado. Our rule was never to teach the same workshop in the same way. We taught simulated television game shows called "guess my rep system" and "groovy deal therapy", a precursor to six step reframing. We had a great time, however our creativity was not always looked upon as genius.

David started an association with Maribeth Anderson. After several trips to visit and study with Milton Erickson they wrote two books together, the most well known being *Phoenix*.

Paul and Steve began a successful partnership that lasted several years. They also followed the road of Milton Erickson and refined and developed a teaching model of hypnosis throughout the United States and set up an Ericksonian Hypnosis Institute in Europe. Steve was very much into modelling Milton.

Milton mentioned that he taught seminars almost every day because it helped him forget the pain that he experienced. He was confined to a wheelchair and would do pain control exercises on himself every morning for a few hours before he taught.

Steve wanted to model Milton so he confined himself to a wheelchair and this was his mode of transportation from class to class at the university. When he found out about this, Milton was very unimpressed by his protege's behaviour, fearing that Steve would develop some of Milton's chronic symptoms. After this Steve limited himself to modelling the gross postures of Milton as well as his numerous communications patterns and therapeutic intervention styles.

Chapter Twenty Seven

NLP Volume One

Robert was commissioned by John and Richard to write *NLP Volume One,* which was later published in 1978. Robert went up to visit John one afternoon and reluctantly let me come along. He was very guarded with his friendship with John. Robert showed John his paper titled *NLP: A New Psychotherapy.* John was impressed to the extent that he then rang up Richard and suggested that Robert assist in writing the book and both John and Richard could serve as supervisors or oversee the written work.

It was initially said that Leslie was supposed to be writing this volume of NLP, however at this time she was more involved in her own work with couple and family therapy and so the commission was given to Robert. As John said, besides Richard owed him a favor for helping get his Bonny Doon house.

The idea of cognitive strategies or the sequences of sensory representational systems came together and the last piece in the NLP puzzle fell into place. Strategies were the next logical sequence of the development of the model of NLP. They happened more as an evolution as opposed to an even.

After the very nature of development of strategies the idea of notation came into effect and, over the next couple of years, notation changed very rapidly.

Strategies have fantastic applications to modelling and education in general. Most people don't take the time to learn them properly because they can't find an immediate application. They would rather do change history or, now days, the swish pattern.

Chapter Twenty Eight

The Untuple/Spinning Out The Belief Strategy

An evening that was a turning point in my understanding of strategies was a visit to Richard at the Bonny Doon house. He was working on techniques to spin out belief strategies. The technique needs to be very thought out before doing. It is one of the few NLP techniques where you cannot predict what the results of your intervention are going to be. It was used when nothing else worked; or in my case if you wanted to find out what would happen if you had your belief strategy spun out.

Richard was telling me that you cannot know where it will lead you if you have never been there. He led me thru a strategy to understand which inevitably led to confusion, at which time he covertly anchored me visually by mimicking my facial expression, facilitated connecting the end of my strategy to the beginning until the strategy was self initiating and I was on my way. Strange colorful dreams and all.

The first thing that happened was I passed my Family Counseling Licensing test under very unusual circumstances. The test was mostly multiple choice and when I didn't know the answer, my internal dialogue would answer a or c. It was as if the person behind was giving me the answers. I had incorporated into consciousness an

auditory representational system which was just the resource I needed. After that, none of the skills that I had made any effect on settling things down. It was a very uncomfortable time for awhile, however one that I would do again, given the opportunity.

NLP is considered now a model in its own, consisting of the meta model, representational systems, anchoring, reframing and strategies.

After the meta model groups, John and Richard began to refine their teaching skills. After a few unsuccessful attempts at teaching the meta model they began to try out new techniques. I remember one time John taught his students at Kresge College the entire meta model in one three hour session. The students learned the meta model, however when they came back they described experiences of losing their friends. The one important component that the students did not consider was the concept of rapport when asking questions.

In one course Richard taught, he spent the entire day eliciting dissatisfaction in the course participants and then spent the entire evening in his hotel room with Robert Dilts designing a model to reframe and install satisfaction back to the group.

Chapter Twenty Nine

The Wedding

John, Richard, Leslie and Judith are booked out continually, either in Santa Cruz or on the road conducting hypnosis or NLP workshops. Another event that occurred in 1977 was that Richard Bandler married Leslie and Leslie Cameron became, Leslie Cameron Bandler. It was by far the gala occasion in Santa Cruz, California. The person who married these two was none other than John Grinder. John was a preacher from the Universal Light Church.

Richard by this time had financial success and purchased and renovated school house in Bonny Doon, California. Over a period of a year, he gradually converted the school house into a mansion complete with swimming pool, spa and tennis court. It was at this house that the wedding took place. Several of the people from the early groups attended as well as personal friends and family of Richard and Leslie.

The marriage took place in the main room of the mansion. John placed himself strategically behind a podium at one end of the main room and placed a large crystal ball in front of the couple. He instructed the couple one at a time to view the crystal ball and see what the future had in store.

If only Richard had known what the crystal ball held in store for him at that time, I'm sure he would have saved himself a lot of money and animosity.

The whole affair was catered by the La Chemire restaurant and copious quantities of champagne flowed all afternoon. Also in attendance were Richard's publisher, Bob Spitzer and Virginia Satir.

Chapter Thirty

DOTAR

Shortly after the wedding, whether on Richard's direction or not, Leslie decided to put together a cadre of NLP'ers. She formed an association with Maribeth Anderson, Robert Dilts, and David Gordon.

Leslie facilitated the purchase of a large facility on Mission Street, Santa Cruz and "Not Limited Division Of Training And Research" of Santa Cruz, California was officially open for business. They presented ongoing workshops, training seminars and Ericksonian Hypnosis programs.

In 1978, Not Limited went into full operation, doing training development and research. The core group now took on assistant trainers who then began putting on workshops and seminars of their own. Frank Pucelik formed a partnership with Byron Lewis who I had taught some training programs with before getting together with Robert Dilts. Frank and Byron coauthored the book *Magic Demystified,* which a lot of people find to be a useful introductory NLP book.

Early in 1978, Steve Stevens became interested in NLP and decided to cease his work in Gestalt Therapy and put all his time and effort into learning the NLP model. I remember Steve when he was a teacher at Diablo Valley Junior College in Concord, California. Steve was a follower of Fritz Perls as was his mother Barry Stevens, who wrote several books, one being a delightful journey called *Don't Push The River*. A wonderful person Barry.

Anyway, Steve's psychology classes were more like Gestalt Groups and I heard that if you cried a lot you got a good grade. So the rumour went anyway. Steve had been together a short time with Connirae when we met, she was finishing up her Ph.D. I believe and doing research regarding couple counseling and the use of predicates.

Steve hired the services of Robert and hence me because I worked with Robert. We had our first gig on the road in Boulder Colorado where Steve was introduced to some of the basic building blocks of NLP and from there, he began following Richard and John from workshop to workshop taping them and then later, editing the transcripts which became the book *Frogs into Princes*. The first NLP book for the layman who knows nothing about psychology or therapy. This was a time of innovation, excitement as well as some confusion and crises.

Chapter Thirty One

This Town Is Too Small

This time period marked another choice point in the development of NLP for Richard and John. In the year of 1978, more tension began to develop between Richard and John and they realized that the stage was not big enough for both of them. For a variety of different reasons, some personal, some business, they decided to go their separate ways. Leslie also at this time was going thru an evolution in her personal life. Personal and business stress affected her and she ended up in hospital for a period of time. Shortly after that she filed for a divorce.

After a few exciting court dealings, Leslie went of with Michael Lebeau, who was later to become her husband, and David Gordon. They set up an organization in Larkspur, California called "Neuro-Linguistic Programming for Advanced Studies". Here the trio continued to promote NLP.

The Society of Neuro-Linguistic Programming formally a partnership between Richard Bandler's company Not Limited and John Grinder's company Unlimited Limited continued to prosper with Richard's guidance. He continued to use the trade mark of the Society of Neuro-Linguistic Programming and eventually bought John out of the Society. They also made new arrangements regarding the publishing company Meta Publications. Richard continued to develop and teach NLP training programs and to be associated with the Society of NLP.

John formed Grinder Delozier and Associates. With one of his associates Michael McMasters he coauthored a book titled *Precision*. John also formed a partnership with Genie Laborde and promoted several Precision workshops across the U.S. John concentrated on the business marketing side of NLP. He utilized his creativity in the refinement of the NLP model with an emphasis on Gregory Bateson's theories on evolutionary communication and Milton Erickson's hypnotic patterns of communication.

Richard, on the other hand, having the belief that people change thru confusion, continued his approach as teacher and developer of change patterns associated with belief models. This later developed in another evolution in NLP which was represented in two books, edited by Steve Andreas. One is called *Using Your Brain For a Change* and the second was from transcripts of therapy sessions into a book called *Magic in Action*.

Robert, after his publication of *NLP Volume 1,* became more and more popular throughout the NLP circuit and began teaching NLP training programs with an emphasis on health models. He kept an association with both Richard Bandler and John Grinder, being a proper Machiavellian as he was.

Judith continued her relationship with John Grinder and they now live in Bonny Doon, just outside of Santa Cruz in the mountains and are continuing to promote and develop John's business.

One thing about NLP is that it was developed under the auspices of practicality, and doing what works. Also preparing people's sensory experience to respond to what was happening at any moment in time. We worked with survival patterns quite often as they are powerful resource states. NLP has been under criticism over the years because of some of the colorful and unscientific procedures that the developers Richard Bandler and John Grinder went thru to design the model. The genius of these two individuals allowed them to step out of the mainstream of what was a scientifically accepted approach.

NLP teaches the individual to respond to their sensory environment. "Anything can happen to anybody at any time in nowhere". I believe that Richard and John prepared for any eventuality. Most of us are well fed, have an income, a car and a stereo. The idea of extreme conflict or violence unless you worked in the CIA or came from the back streets of east San Jose or served in the Vietnam war, is not a normal perception that we grow up with. In some areas of the world the idea of extreme conflict or violence is normal activity from day to day, and people grow up and are taught to cope with this from very early ages. The point is, be prepared.

NLP teaches us the niceties of rapport as well as teaching us how to cope with things that are not so pleasant. More than a few of the workshop exercises that we participated in had to do with eliciting responses in people that had to do with survival or coping patterns, periods of violence, being able to deal with dangerous situations, and applying those resources in problematic situations, as resource anchors.

Chapter Thirty Two

Operationalising NLP

In 1978 and 1979, the patterns of NLP began to be applied to areas outside of the therapeutic framework. The application of the patterns of NLP was called "Operationalising NLP": putting NLP patterns into a variety of different contexts to test the validity and success. On one occasion, John Grinder referred a client, who was a millionaire from the midwest, to Robert and I. John gave us a task to determine if NLP could be applied on the community level in order to assist a person to change. Our task was to operationalise the NLP patterns in the context of the town of Santa Cruz.

We were to work with this individual, who we will give the name of Morty, for twelve hours a day, for five days and to teach him public speaking, assertiveness and generally build his self esteem. We devised a strategic plan to go about changing Morty the millionaire from a waddling duck to a boardroom supervisor of a hotel chain.

We began our work at 7.30 in the morning, with vigorous exercise, and then took him out on the town for a variety of tasks which took in the next twelve hours. Later on these exercises were called "Tasks on the Town" and became common place in NLP workshops.

Some of the tasks that we designed were conducted in the following manner. For example, on one occasion Morty said that he had a fear of someone calling him a homosexual. So we set about having him go out and buy twenty four red roses and stand on the street corner and sell them to individuals. Sure enough some yahoo came up and called him a "fairy". His task was then to go about eliciting friendship from this individual.

The next task was to have another individual come up and say he had actually known Morty from his mid west home city. The Santa Cruzen happened to be a derelict type and completely confused Morty. The purpose was to elicit temporary confusion and question the client's personal credibility.

Another technique which was designed to elicit an assertive response from the client, was to let the client know that anything could happen and at any time. Santa Cruz was then known as the murder capital of the world because of a recent mass slaying that took place in the mountains. So this statement was not altogether untrue.

At eight o'clock one morning, Robert took Morty for a jog on the beach. Waiting for the client to pass a certain area on the beach was another person who was a scruffy workman type. This person came up to Morty and accosted him to determine if he could elicit an assertive response which would then later be utilized as a survival pattern for the client.

These kinds of activities went on for five days. Either Robert or I would go down to the streets of Santa Cruz and find an appropriate individual to commission for a small fee to be an actor or actress in the drama using Santa Cruz as the stage to be able to elicit behaviour patterns from Morty.

The final task was to be able to determine that once the person had changed would the patterns continue even in an altered state of consciousness. Robert and I took the millionaire to Santa Cruz Bar and Grill, one of the finer restaurants in town and after a very fine dinner, having achieved an altered state of consciousness in Morty, we set about to discover if he had access to his survival skills in an altered state of consciousness.

One of the patterns that the millionaire wanted to change was at times he broke out into fits of anger and rage for very ordinary reasons. So it was at a time when everybody else had left the table except for Morty and I, that I took a hot cup of steaming coffee and looked at Morty meaningfully in the eyes and strategically spilled it in his lap. After he had changed about four different colors, he gracefully excused himself and went of to the men's room, to brush off his blue pinstriped suit.

The results of these exercises were to be known the very next morning. I met Morty first thing in the morning and was delighted when he shook my hand and thanked me for everything that I had done.

The exercises were not completed however and the next thing that Robert did was to get on the same airplane that Morty the millionaire was on and fly back to the mid west. Robert then preceded to go to Morty's home and his place of business with him, to ensure that the patterns were not only useful and working in Santa Cruz, but were also available and installed in the context that he would be using them. A very sophisticated and expensive future pacing.

Epilogue

It was activities like these where students utilized the patterns of NLP to their fullest potential and began to develop the flexibility of the model in a variety of contexts. It is now beginning to be used in the classrooms across the U.S. The ideas of learning strategies are becoming known to some teachers and in the late eighties educational systems will be spending millions of dollars to retrain their teachers in the NLP technology. Insurance companies, recruiters and manufacturers will be spending twenty times as much to apply NLP to management, sales, service and new product development.

The U.S. army will apply the NLP modelling technology to sharpshooter, hovercraft and helicopter pilot training. Foreign nations will add NLP techniques to their commando training. College professors will continue to denounce NLP and the claims of its practitioners and make passionate speeches about its unscientific approach in the learned halls around the world. NLP will be taught in virtually every English speaking country in the world. Other university teachers will be adding it to their course curriculums and NLP practitioners around the world in virtually every context that involves face to face or telephone conversation will be doing "MAGIC"

About The Author

Terrence Lee McClendon was born in Albany, California. In 1971, he was an undergraduate student at the University of California, Santa Cruz. He graduated in 1973 and went on to gain his Masters Degree in counselling psychology. Throughout the seventies, he worked as a counsellor and trainer for family services and counselling centres.

In 1979, Terry was invited to teach NLP in Sydney, Australia. After many return trips, he settled in Australia and founded the Australian Institute of Neuro-Linguistic Programming. He conducts public seminars and inhouse company training for organisations internationally. He is a Registered Psychologist and Master Trainer with the Society of Neuro-Linguistic Programming. Terry has also designed and developed computerised personality assessment software and produced video training aids.

His joys in life are his lover and their baby daughter, teaching and counselling, wood working, scuba diving and travelling.

Bibliography

Bandler, Richard and Grinder, John. *Frogs Into Princes.* Real People Press, 1979.
Bandler, Richard. *Magic In Action.* Meta Publications, 1984.
Bandler, Richard and Grinder, John. Original Notes (Source T. McClendon) Workshops from 1972 to 1975.
Bandler, Richard and Grinder, John. *The Structure of Magic I.* Science and Behaviour Books, 1975.
Bandler, Richard. *Using Your Brain - for a Change.* Meta Publications, 1985.
Castaneda, Carlos. *A Separate Reality.* Penguin Books Limited, 1971.
Castaneda, Carlos. *The Teachings of don Juan: a Yaqui Way of Knowledge.* Ballantine Books, 1968.
Dilts, Robert; Grinder, John; Bandler, Richard; Delozier, Judith and Cameron-Bandler, Leslie. *Neuro-Linguistic Programming I.* Meta Publications, 1979.
Gordon, David. *Therapeutic Metaphors: Helping Others Through the Looking Glass.* Meta Publications, 1978.
Gordon, David and Meyers-Anderson, Maribeth. *Phoenix, Therapeutic Patterns of Milton H. Erickson.* Meta Publications, 1981.
Grinder, John and Bandler, Richard. *The Structure of Magic II.* Science and Behaviour Books, 1976.
Grinder, John and Bandler, Richard. *Trance-formations: Neuro-Linguistic Programming and the Structure of Hypnosis.* Real People Press, 1981.
Lewis, Byron and Pucelik, Frank. *Magic Demystified.* Metamorphous Press.
Perls, Fritz. *The Gestalt Approach and Eye Witness to Therapy.* Science & Behaviour Books, 1973.
Satir, Virginia. *Conjoint Family Therapy.* Science and Behaviour Books, 1967.
Satir, Virginia. Original Notes (Source T. McClendon). Cold Mountain Workshops.

Made in the USA
San Bernardino, CA
23 January 2015